PIZZA

TOPPINGS

❧

60 easy recipes
for making good food fast

HAMLYN

First published in Great Britain in 1994 by
Hamlyn, an imprint of Reed Consumer Books Limited
Michelin House, 81 Fulham Road, London SW3 6RB
and Auckland, Melbourne, Singapore and Toronto

ISBN 0-600-58258-2

A CIP catalogue record for this book
is available from the British Library

ACKNOWLEDGEMENTS
Designed and produced by: The Bridgewater Book Company
Series Editors: Veronica Sperling and Christine McFadden
Art Director: Peter Bridgewater
Designer: Terry Jeavons
Photography: Trevor Wood
Food preparation and styling: Jonathan Higgins
Cookery contributor: Christine McFadden

Produced by Mandarin Offset
Printed and bound in Singapore

NOTES

❦ Standard level spoon measurements are used in all recipes.

❦ Both imperial and metric measurements have been given in all
recipes. Use one set of measurements only and not a mixture of both.

❦ Eggs should be size 3 unless otherwise stated.

❦ Milk should be full fat unless otherwise stated.

❦ Fresh herbs should be used unless otherwise stated. If unavailable use
dried herbs as an alternative but halve the quantites stated.

❦ Ovens should be preheated to the specified temperature - if using a
fan assisted oven, follow manufacturer's instructions for adjusting the
time and the temperature.

❦ All microwave information is based on a 650 watt oven. Follow
manufacturer's instructions for an oven with a different wattage.

Contents

Introduction

*T*HERE is nothing to beat the irresistible aroma and taste of a crisp chewy pizza baked in a wood-fired brick oven. However, with the right equipment, good quality ingredients, and a little practice, delicious pizzas can be made at home.

The secret is to bake the pizzas at a very high temperature at the top of a preheated oven, for as short a time as possible. Baking on a pizza stone produces the crispest results, because of the direct heat from the stone. Alternatively, use a perforated pizza pan – the holes allow heat and air to reach the centre of the base, resulting in a crisp, evenly cooked crust. Small pizzas will bake reasonably well on a baking sheet.

Although pizza is a simple dish, success depends on using the best quality, freshest ingredients. Good olive oil is essential – 'extra virgin' has the fruitiest flavour, 'pure' olive oil is lighter. Use grapeseed or sunflower oil for greasing pans. Always use freshly grated Parmesan cheese and freshly ground black pepper. Use fresh herbs unless otherwise stated. If they are unavailable, use half the quantity of dried herbs.

Pizza Dough

The dough recipes make enough for either one 30 cm/12 inch pizza, two 20 cm/8 inch pizzas, four 15 cm/6 inch pizzas or six 12.5 cm/5 inch pizzas.

The amount of liquid required depends on the type and quality of the flour, and the amount of moisture in the air.

In some cases, the dough specified goes particularly well with the topping, but in general the types of dough are interchangeable between the recipes.

Basic Pizza Dough

225 g/8 oz unbleached strong plain flour	1 tsp salt
1 tsp easy-blend dried yeast (½ sachet)	1 tbsp olive oil
	125–150 ml/4 fl oz–¼ pint tepid water

*S*IFT the flour, yeast and salt into a bowl. Make a well in the centre and pour in the oil and water. Stir vigorously, gradually drawing in the flour, to form a soft dough. Knead for at least 10 minutes until the dough feels silky smooth and springy.

❧ Place in an oiled bowl, turning once so the surface is coated. Cover with cling film and leave to rise in a warm place for 1-2 hours until doubled in size.

Wholemeal Pizza Dough

150g/5 oz strong wholemeal flour	1 tsp salt
75 g/3 oz unbleached strong	1 tbsp olive oil
plain flour	125-150 ml/4fl oz-¼ pint
1 tsp easy-blend dried yeast	tepid water
(½ sachet)	

$\mathscr{S}$IFT the flours, yeast and salt, adding to the bowl the bran from the wholemeal flour. Make a well in the centre and pour in the oil and water. Stir vigorously, gradually drawing in the flour, to form a soft dough. Knead for at least 10 minutes until the dough feels smooth, elastic and springy.
❦ Place in an oiled bowl, turning once so the surface is coated. Cover with cling film and leave to rise in a warm place for about 1½ hours until doubled in size.

Rich Pizza Dough

225 g/8 oz unbleached strong	5 tbsp tepid milk
plain flour	1 large egg, beaten
1 sachet easy-blend dried yeast	4 tbsp tepid olive oil
1 tsp salt	

$\mathscr{S}$IFT the flour, yeast and salt into a warmed bowl. Make a well in the centre and pour in the milk, egg and oil. Stir vigorously, gradually drawing in the flour, to form a soft dough. Knead for at least 10 minutes until smooth and springy.
❦ Place in an oiled bowl, turning once so the surface is coated. Cover with cling film and leave to rise in a warm place for 1–2 hours until doubled in size.

Tomato Sauce

MAKES 175–225 ML/6–8 FL OZ

3 tbsp olive oil	1 tsp dried oregano
400 g/14 oz can chopped	pinch of sugar
tomatoes	salt and freshly ground black pepper

$\mathscr{P}$UT all the ingredients in a pan and bring to the boil. Simmer briskly for 20–25 minutes until very thick.

Flavoured Oils

Brushing the dough all over with garlic or chilli oil provides extra flavour, and helps keep the dough crisp.
GARLIC OIL: put a few chopped roasted or raw garlic cloves in a screw-top jar and cover with good quality olive oil.
CHILLI OIL: mix 1 teaspoon of chilli powder, or 1–2 roasted fresh chillies, with 150 ml/¼ pint of good quality olive oil.

Spinach and Ricotta Pizza Squares

MAKES ABOUT 28 SQUARES

50 g/2 oz cooked spinach, drained
thoroughly
50 g/2 oz ricotta cheese, sieved
75 g/3 oz freshly grated Parmesan
cheese

2 quantities Basic Pizza Dough
1 egg white, lightly whisked
oil, for deep-frying

*P*URÉE the spinach in an electric blender or food processor. Combine with the ricotta and Parmesan cheeses.

❧ Roll out the dough to a 35.5 × 40 cm/14 × 16 inch rectangle. Using a tooth-edged rotary cutter, cut the rectangle into 5 cm/2 inch squares.

❧ Place 1 teaspoon of spinach mixture in the centre of half the squares. Brush the edges with whisked egg white, and cover with the remaining squares, pressing the edges together firmly to seal.

❧ Heat the oil in a deep-fryer to 180–190°C/350–375°F or until a cube of bread turns golden in 30 seconds. Fry the squares, a few at a time, until golden. Drain on absorbent kitchen paper, and serve immediately.

Goat Cheese and Roasted Pepper Pizzette

MAKES FOUR 15 CM/6 INCH PIZZAS

1 red and 1 yellow pepper
2 garlic cloves, unskinned
1 quantity Basic Pizza Dough
Chilli Oil, for brushing
175 g/6 oz mozzarella cheese, grated

75 g/3 oz dry goat cheese, crumbled
8 pitted black olives, sliced
freshly ground black pepper
oregano leaves, to garnish

*P*LACE the peppers and garlic cloves on a greased baking sheet. Bake in a preheated oven at 200°C/400°F/gas mark 6 for 20 minutes. Remove the skins from the peppers and garlic. Slice the peppers very thinly and mash the garlic.

❧ Roll out the dough to four 15 cm/6 inch circles. Transfer to greased perforated pizza pans. Brush with chilli oil, and smear with the garlic.

❧ Sprinkle the mozzarella cheese over the dough, then arrange the peppers, goat cheese and olives on top. Season with pepper.

❧ Bake in a preheated oven at 240°C/475°F/gas mark 9 for 25 minutes until the cheese is bubbling. Garnish with oregano leaves, and serve at once.

Radicchio and Artichoke Pizza

MAKES TWO 20 CM/8 INCH PIZZAS

1 head radicchio, leaves separated
1 quantity Basic Pizza Dough
walnut oil, for brushing
4 bottled artichoke hearts, quartered
6 walnut halves, chopped roughly

100 g/4 oz gorgonzola cheese,
cut into 1.5 cm/½ inch dice
freshly ground black pepper
marjoram leaves, to garnish

PLUNGE the radicchio leaves into boiling water for 30 seconds. Drain under cold running water, and dry thoroughly on absorbent kitchen paper. Roughly chop the larger leaves.

❧ Roll out the dough to two 20 cm/8 inch circles. Place on greased perforated pizza pans.

❧ Brush with walnut oil. Arrange the radicchio on top, turning the leaves so that they are coated with oil. Add the artichokes, walnuts and gorgonzola cheese. Season with pepper.

❧ Bake in a preheated oven at 240°C/475°F/gas mark 9 for 15 minutes. Garnish with marjoram, and serve at once.

Aubergine and Red Pepper Pizza

MAKES TWO 20 CM/8 INCH PIZZAS

1 small aubergine, thinly sliced
1 red pepper, seeded and halved
2 large garlic cloves, unskinned
Chilli Oil, for brushing
1 quantity Basic Pizza Dough

75 g/3 oz mozzarella cheese, grated
75 g/3 oz dry goat cheese, crumbled
salt and freshly ground black pepper
oregano leaves, to garnish

PLACE the aubergine, peppers and garlic cloves on a greased baking sheet. Brush the aubergine slices with chilli oil. Bake in a preheated oven at 200°C/400°F/gas mark 6 ,for 20 minutes, turning the aubergine slices once and brushing with chilli oil.

❧ Remove the skins from the peppers and garlic. Thinly slice the peppers, and mash the garlic.

❧ Roll out the dough to two 20 cm/8 inch circles. Transfer to greased perforated pizza pans.

❧ Brush with chilli oil, and smear with garlic.

❧ Sprinkle with the mozzarella cheese, and arrange the aubergine slices and peppers on top. Add the goat cheese, season to taste, and sprinkle with chilli oil.

❧ Bake in a preheated oven at 240°C/475°F/gas mark 9 for about 15 minutes. Garnish with oregano, and serve at once.

Pizza Nera e Bianca
(Black and White Pizza)

MAKES TWO 20 CM/8 INCH PIZZAS

1 quantity Basic Pizza Dough
6 tbsp tapenade (olive paste)
1 tsp dried oregano

100 g/4 oz mozzarella cheese, sliced
basil leaves, to garnish

*R*OLL out the dough to two 20 cm/8 inch circles. Transfer to greased perforated pizza pans.

❧ Spread with the tapenade, and sprinkle with the oregano. Arrange the mozzarella slices on top.

❧ Bake in a preheated oven at 240°C/475°F/gas mark 9 for 10–12 minutes. Garnish with basil leaves, and serve at once.

Sfinciuno with Broccoli, Yellow Pepper and Ricotta
(Sicilian Stuffed Pizza)

MAKES ONE 30 CM/12 INCH DOUBLE–CRUSTED SFINCIUNO

1 tbsp olive oil
1 large yellow pepper,
    seeded and diced
1 garlic clove, finely chopped
450 g/1 lb broccoli florets,
    2.5 cm/1 inch diameter, blanched
    and drained
grated zest of ½ lemon

salt and freshly ground black pepper
275 g/9 oz ricotta cheese, sieved
1–2 tbsp milk
2 quantities Rich Pizza Dough
4 tbsp toasted breadcrumbs
4 tbsp freshly grated Parmesan
    cheese

*H*EAT the oil and stir-fry the pepper until softened. Add the garlic and fry until just coloured. Remove from the pan, and combine with the broccoli, lemon zest and seasoning.

❧ Mix the ricotta to a spreading consistency with the milk.

❧ Divide the dough in two. Roll out to a 33 cm/13 inch circle, and a 30 cm/12 inch circle. Place the larger circle on a greased perforated pizza pan. Brush with oil, leaving a 1 cm/½ inch border round the edge.

❧ Sprinkle with half the breadcrumbs and spread the ricotta on top. Add the broccoli mixture, and season to taste. Sprinkle with the Parmesan, remaining breadcrumbs and some olive oil.

❧ Place the other circle on top. Dampen the edges with water. Bring up the edges of the lower circle, and seal. Brush with oil.

❧ Bake in an oven preheated to 200°C/400°F/gas mark 6 for 25–30 minutes, until golden and the base is cooked.

Mushroom, Goat Cheese and Radicchio Calzoni
(Pizza Turnovers)

MAKES 4 CALZONI

350 g/12 oz assorted wild or cultivated mushrooms, chopped into even-sized pieces
3 tbsp olive oil
2 garlic cloves, finely chopped
2 tbsp finely chopped fresh thyme

salt and freshly ground black pepper
½ head radicchio, leaves separated, blanched and dried
1 quantity Basic Pizza Dough
100 g/4 oz dry goat cheese, crumbled
freshly grated Parmesan cheese

*S*TIR-FRY the mushrooms in the oil for about 5 minutes. Add the garlic, thyme and seasoning, and fry for another minute. Transfer to a bowl. Roughly chop the radicchio, and add to the mushrooms.

❧ On a well-floured surface, roll out the dough to four 15 cm/6 inch circles. Brush the centres with oil, and dampen the edges.

❧ Place a little mushroom mixture on one half of each circle, leaving a 1 cm/½ inch border. Sprinkle with the goat cheese.

❧ Fold the circles over, pinching the edges together to seal. Brush all over with oil, and transfer to a greased perforated pizza pan. Leave to rise in a warm place for 30 minutes.

❧ Bake in a preheated oven at 240°C/475°F/gas mark 9 for 15–20 minutes until golden brown. Brush with oil, sprinkle with Parmesan cheese and serve immediately.

Red Pepper and Onion Pizza

MAKES TWO 20 CM/8 INCH PIZZAS

2 tbsp olive oil
1 large red onion, thinly sliced
1 large red pepper, seeded and thinly sliced
1 tbsp finely chopped fresh rosemary
salt and freshly ground black pepper

1 quantity Basic Wholemeal Pizza Dough
4 tbsp tapenade (olive paste)
225 g/8 oz mozzarella cheese, thinly sliced
basil leaves, to garnish

*H*EAT the oil and gently fry the onion, peppers and rosemary for 5–7 minutes. Season to taste.

❧ Roll out the dough to two 20 cm/8 inch circles. Transfer to greased perforated pizza pans.

❧ Spread with the tapenade. Top with the onion mixture and sprinkle with the mozzarella cheese.

❧ Bake in a preheated oven at 240°C/475°F/gas mark 9 for 15 minutes. Garnish with torn basil leaves, and serve at once.

Aubergine and Tomato Pizza

MAKES ONE 30 CM/12 INCH PIZZA

4–6 tbsp olive oil
1 aubergine, sliced
salt and freshly ground black pepper
1 quantity Basic Pizza Dough
1 quantity Tomato Sauce

175 g/6 oz mozzarella cheese,
  thinly sliced
4 tbsp freshly grated Parmesan
  cheese

*H*EAT 4 tablespoons of the oil in a frying pan, and fry the aubergine in batches until brown on both sides. Add more oil to the pan as necessary. Drain the aubergine slices on absorbent kitchen paper. Season to taste.

❧ Roll out the dough to a 30 cm/12 inch circle, and place on a greased perforated pizza pan.

❧ Spread the tomato sauce evenly over the dough, and arrange the aubergine slices on top. Cover with the slices of mozzarella.

❧ Bake in a preheated oven at 240°C/475°F/gas mark 9 for 15–20 minutes. Sprinkle with Parmesan cheese, and serve immediately.

Cheese, Tomato and Garlic Pizza

MAKES TWO 20 CM/8 INCH PIZZAS

1 quantity Basic Pizza Dough
Garlic Oil, for brushing
400 g/14 oz can chopped tomatoes,
  drained
salt and freshly ground black pepper
2 tsp dried oregano

225 g/8 oz mozzarella cheese,
  thinly sliced
4 tbsp freshly grated Parmesan
  cheese
basil leaves, to garnish

*R*OLL out the dough to two 20 cm/8 inch circles. Place on greased perforated pizza pans.

❧ Brush with garlic oil and spread the chopped tomatoes evenly over the dough. Season to taste and sprinkle with the oregano. Add the mozzarella slices, and top with the Parmesan cheese. Drizzle with garlic oil.

❧ Bake in a preheated oven at 240°C/475°F/gas mark 9 for 15 minutes. Garnish with torn basil leaves, and serve at once.

Pizza alla Napoletana

MAKES ONE 30 CM/12 INCH PIZZA

1 quantity Basic Pizza Dough
olive oil, for brushing
450 g/1 lb tomatoes, peeled,
   roughly chopped and drained
1 garlic clove, finely chopped
salt and freshly ground black pepper

225 g/8 oz mozzarella cheese,
   thinly sliced
6 anchovy fillets, split lengthways
1 tbsp finely chopped fresh basil
   or oregano

ROLL out the dough to a 30 cm/12 inch circle, and place on a greased perforated pizza pan. Brush with olive oil.

❧ Mix together the tomatoes, garlic and seasoning, and spread the mixture evenly over the dough. Top with the cheese and the anchovy fillets and sprinkle with basil or oregano. Drizzle with olive oil.

❧ Bake in a preheated oven at 240°C/475°F/gas mark 9 for 15–20 minutes. Serve immediately, cut into wedges.

VARIATION: For Pizza alla Siciliana, omit the mozzarella cheese, and add 50 g/2 oz pitted black olives, roughly chopped.

Mushroom and Onion Pizza

MAKES ONE 30 CM/12 INCH PIZZA

4 tbsp olive oil
2 onions, thinly sliced
350 g/12 oz mushrooms, thinly sliced
2 garlic cloves, finely chopped
3 tbsp finely chopped fresh
   mixed herbs

salt and freshly ground black pepper
10 pitted black olives
1 quantity Basic Pizza Dough
4 tbsp freshly grated Parmesan
   cheese

HEAT the oil in a frying pan, and gently fry the onions for 5 minutes, until softened. Add the mushrooms and garlic, and cook for a further 5–7 minutes, until the juices have evaporated. Stir in the herbs and season to taste.

❧ Roll out the dough to a 30 cm/12 inch circle, and place on a greased perforated pizza pan.

❧ Spread the mushroom mixture evenly over the dough, and top with the olives.

❧ Bake in a preheated oven at 240°C/475°F/gas mark 9 for 15–20 minutes. Sprinkle with Parmesan cheese and serve immediately.

Mushroom and Garlic Pizzette

MAKES FOUR 12.5 CM/5 INCH PIZZAS

6 tbsp olive oil
4 large garlic cloves, skinned
   and left whole
350 g/12 oz mushrooms, thinly sliced
salt and freshly ground black pepper

1 quantity Basic Pizza Dough
1½ tbsp finely chopped fresh
   rosemary
6 tbsp freshly grated Parmesan
   cheese

*H*EAT half the olive oil in a small frying pan. Gently fry the garlic cloves over a low heat until golden. Reserving the oil, remove the garlic, allow to cool, then slice thinly.

❧ Heat the remaining oil in a large pan, and stir-fry the mushrooms until the juices have evaporated. Season to taste.

❧ Roll out the dough to four 12.5 cm cm/5 inch circles. Transfer to a greased perforated pizza pan.

❧ Brush with the reserved garlic cooking oil, and sprinkle with garlic and rosemary. Top with the mushrooms and Parmesan.

❧ Bake in a preheated oven at 240°C/475°F/gas mark 9 for 12–15 minutes, until bubbling. Serve at once.

Three-Cheese Pizza

MAKES ONE 20 CM/8 INCH PIZZA

350 g/12 oz strong plain flour
1 sachet easy-blend dried yeast
½ tsp salt
125 ml/4 fl oz tepid water
90 g/3½ oz Parmesan cheese

90 g/3½ oz gruyère cheese
40 g/1½ oz pecorino cheese
2 eggs, beaten
olive oil, for brushing
dried oregano, to garnish

*S*IFT 100 g/4 oz of flour into a bowl, with the yeast and salt. Stir in 4–5 tablespoons of tepid water and knead until smooth. Place in a large oiled bowl, cover with cling film, and leave to rise in a warm place for 15 minutes.

❧ Grate 50 g/2 oz of the Parmesan and half the gruyère cheese. Dice the remaining cheese, and add to the grated cheese. Stir in the eggs and the remaining flour. Mix in the remaining water.

❧ Add the first ball of dough to the cheese mixture, and knead for at least 10 minutes until no longer sticky. Return to the bowl, cover, and leave to rise for 1–2 hours.

❧ Roll out to a 20 cm/8 inch circle. Place on a greased perforated pizza pan, and leave to rise for 40 minutes.

❧ Bake in a preheated oven at 200°C/400°F/gas mark 6 for 20–25 minutes.

❧ Brush with oil, sprinkle with oregano, and serve immediately.

Cheese and Chilli Calzoni
(Pizza Turnovers)

MAKES 4 CALZONI

1 red and 1 yellow pepper
2 large garlic cloves, unskinned
1–2 fresh green or red chillies
8 pitted black olives, sliced
50 g/2 oz smoked cheese, diced
50 g/2 oz mozzarella cheese, diced

6 tbsp freshly grated Parmesan
   cheese
2 tbsp finely chopped fresh
   coriander or flat-leafed parsley
1 quantity Basic Pizza Dough
olive oil, for brushing

PLACE the peppers, garlic cloves and chillies on a greased baking sheet. Bake in a preheated oven at 200°C/400°F/gas mark 6 for 15–20 minutes.

❦ Remove all the skins, and seed the peppers and chillies. Cut the peppers into 1.5 cm /½ inch squares, and chop the chillies and garlic. Combine with the olives, smoked and mozzarella cheeses, and half the Parmesan cheese.

❦ Roll out the dough to four 15 cm/6 inch circles. Brush the centre of each circle with olive oil, and brush the edges with water. Place some of the filling on one half of each circle.

❦ Fold the circles over, pinching the edges together to seal. Brush with oil and transfer to a greased perforated pizza pan. Leave in a warm place to rise for 30 minutes.

❦ Bake in a preheated oven at 240°C/475°F/gas mark 9 for 15–20 minutes until golden brown. Brush with oil, sprinkle with the remaining Parmesan cheese, and serve immediately.

Olive and Herb Deep Pan Pizza

MAKES ONE 28 CM/11 INCH PIZZA

1 quantity Rich Pizza Dough
2 quantities Tomato Sauce
4 tbsp finely chopped fresh herbs
   e.g. basil, thyme, chives, marjoram

150 g/5 oz green and black oil-cured
   olives, pitted
olive oil, for brushing

ROLL out the dough and use to line a 28 cm/11 inch round flan tin. Prick the base, and bake in a preheated oven at 240°C/475°F/gas mark 9 for 7 minutes.

❦ Pour the tomato sauce into the flan case, and scatter over the herbs. Arrange the olives on top, and drizzle with olive oil.

❦ Lower the oven temperature to 180°C/350°F/gas mark 4, and bake for a further 10–15 minutes. Serve immediately.

Pine Nut Pizza

MAKES TWO 20 CM/8 INCH PIZZAS

2 tbsp olive oil
2 onions, thinly sliced
1 red pepper, seeded and sliced
salt and freshly ground black pepper
1 quantity Basic Pizza Dough
100 g/4 oz mozzarella cheese, sliced

25 g/1 oz pine nuts
2 tbsp freshly grated Parmesan
   cheese
basil leaves, to garnish

*H*EAT the oil in a frying pan, and gently fry the onions for 5 minutes. Add the pepper, season and cook for a further 5 minutes, until the onions are softened and lightly coloured. Remove from the heat and allow to cool.

❧ Roll out the dough to two 20 cm/8 inch circles. Place the circles on greased perforated pizza pans.

❧ Spread the onion mixture evenly over the dough. Arrange the mozzarella cheese on top, and sprinkle with the pine nuts. Top with the Parmesan cheese.

❧ Bake in a preheated oven at 240°C/475°F/gas mark 9 for 15–20 minutes. Garnish with basil leaves, and serve at once.

Deep Pan Spinach Pizza
with Sun-Dried Tomatoes

MAKES ONE 28 CM/11 INCH PIZZA

1 quantity Rich Pizza Dough
Garlic Oil, for brushing
700 g/1½ lb spinach, stems removed
1 quantity Tomato Sauce
salt and freshly ground black pepper

6 sun-dried tomatoes, chopped
175 g/6 oz mozzarella cheese,
   grated
50 g/2 oz Parmesan cheese,
   freshly grated

*R*OLL out the dough to fit a 28 cm/11 inch greased flan tin, pressing it well into the base and sides. Trim the edge and prick the base. Bake in a preheated oven at 240°C/475°F/ gas mark 9 for 7 minutes. Brush all over with garlic oil.

❧ Wash the spinach and put in a saucepan without any extra water. Cover and simmer until just tender, stirring frequently. Drain and press out all the moisture, then chop roughly.

❧ Spread the dough with the tomato sauce, and top with the spinach. Season to taste. Sprinkle with the mozzarella cheese, sun-dried tomatoes, half the Parmesan, and a little olive oil.

❧ Bake for 20 minutes, until the base is cooked through. Sprinkle with the remaining Parmesan cheese and serve.

Pissaladière

MAKES ONE 25 × 35.5 CM/10 × 14 INCH PIZZA

4 tbsp olive oil
4 onions, thinly sliced
2 garlic cloves, finely chopped
2 tbsp finely chopped fresh thyme
freshly ground black pepper
1 quantity Rich Pizza Dough

1 quantity Tomato Sauce
2 × 50 g/2 oz cans anchovy fillets,
  drained
12–15 black olives, pitted
thyme sprigs, to garnish

*H*EAT the oil in a large pan, and gently fry the onions, garlic and thyme, for 15 minutes, until the onions are pale golden. Season with freshly ground black pepper.

❧ Roll out the dough to fit a 25 × 35.5 cm/10 × 14 inch greased Swiss roll tin.

❧ Spread with the tomato sauce. Bake in a preheated oven at 240°C/475°F/gas mark 9 for 5 minutes.

❧ Remove from the oven, and top with the onion mixture. Arrange the anchovy fillets in a lattice pattern, and place an olive in the centre of each square.

❧ Bake for 15 minutes more. Garnish with thyme sprigs, and serve warm or cold.

Roasted Pepper and Olive Pizza

MAKES ONE 25 × 35.5 CM/10 × 14 INCH PIZZA

2 small red, yellow and
  green peppers
1 quantity Basic Wholemeal
  Pizza Dough
1 quantity Tomato Sauce
salt and freshly ground black pepper

½ tbsp dried oregano
75 g/3 oz mozzarella cheese, grated
3 tbsp freshly grated Parmesan
  cheese
12 black olives, pitted

*P*LACE the peppers on a greased baking sheet. Bake in a preheated oven at 200°C/400°F/gas mark 6 until the skins begin to blacken. Remove the skins and seeds, and roughly chop the flesh, keeping the colours separate.

❧ Roll out the dough to fit a 25 × 35.5 cm/10 × 14 inch greased Swiss roll tin. Spread with the tomato sauce.

❧ Bake in a preheated oven at 240°C/475°F/gas mark 9 for 5 minutes. Remove from the oven, and arrange the peppers on top in diagonal stripes of alternating colours. Season to taste and sprinkle with the oregano. Top with the mozzarella and Parmesan cheeses, and finish with the olives.

❧ Bake for 15 minutes more, and serve at once.

Three-Onion Pizza

MAKES TWO 20 CM/8 INCH PIZZAS

3 red onions, thinly sliced lengthways
3 tbsp olive oil
2 garlic cloves, finely chopped
1 tbsp finely chopped fresh rosemary
salt and freshly ground black pepper
1 quantity Rich Pizza Dough
1 quantity Tomato Sauce

225 g/8 oz mozzarella cheese, grated
8 spring onions, chopped
2 tbsp crispy dried onions
6 tbsp freshly grated Parmesan
  cheese
chopped spring onion tops, to garnish

GENTLY fry the red onions in the oil for 5 minutes. Add the garlic and rosemary, season to taste, and gently fry for another 3–5 minutes until soft.

❧ Roll out the dough to two 20 cm/8 inch circles. Transfer to greased perforated pizza pans.

❧ Spread the dough with the tomato sauce, cooked onions, mozzarella cheese, and spring onions. Drizzle with olive oil.

❧ Bake in a preheated oven at 240°C/475°F/gas mark 9 for 15 minutes.

❧ Sprinkle with the dried onions and Parmesan cheese. Garnish with spring onion tops and serve at once.

Red Onion and Pine Nut Pizza

MAKES ONE 30 CM/12 INCH PIZZA

6 tbsp olive oil
4 red onions, thinly sliced
3 large garlic cloves, thinly sliced
1 tbsp balsamic vinegar
2 tbsp finely chopped fresh thyme
salt and freshly ground black pepper

1 quantity Basic Pizza Dough
1 quantity Tomato Sauce
100 g/4 oz feta cheese
25 g/1 oz pine nuts
thyme sprigs, to garnish

HEAT the oil in a large frying pan, and fry the onions over a very low heat for about 30 minutes, stirring occasionally.

❧ Raise the heat, add the garlic and fry until pale golden. Stir in the vinegar and thyme, and season generously. Remove from the pan with a slotted spoon.

❧ Roll out the dough to a 30 cm/12 inch circle. Place on a greased perforated pizza pan.

❧ Spread the tomato sauce over the dough, followed by the onions. Sprinkle with the feta cheese and pine nuts.

❧ Bake in a preheated oven at 240°C/475°F/gas mark 9 for 12–15 minutes. Garnish with thyme sprigs, and serve at once.

Calzoni alla Napoletana
(Pizza Turnovers)

MAKES 6 CALZONI

1 quantity Basic Pizza Dough
olive oil, for brushing
4 tomatoes, peeled, seeded, chopped, and drained

6 small slices of mozzarella cheese
6 anchovy fillets
salt and freshly ground black pepper
oil, for deep-frying

*D*IVIDE the pizza dough into six equal portions. Roll out to thin 13 cm/5 inch circles. Brush the centre of each circle with the olive oil, and brush the edges with water.

❧ Place a little chopped tomato, a slice of mozzarella cheese and an anchovy fillet on one half of each circle, and season to taste. Fold the circles over, and pinch the edges together.

❧ Place the turnovers on a floured baking sheet, cover with a clean cloth and leave in a warm place for 30 minutes.

❧ Heat the oil in a deep-fryer to 180–190°C/300–375°F or until a cube of bread turns golden in 30 seconds. Deep-fry the calzoni for 5–6 minutes until crisp and golden. Drain well and serve at once.

Mushroom and Green Pepper Pizza

MAKES TWO 20 CM/8 INCH PIZZAS

3 tbsp olive oil
350 g/12 oz button mushrooms, sliced
1 garlic clove, finely chopped
salt and freshly ground black pepper
1 quantity Basic Pizza Dough
1 quantity Tomato Sauce

1 green pepper, seeded and thinly sliced
4 tbsp freshly grated Parmesan cheese
basil leaves, to garnish

*H*EAT the oil in a frying pan and stir-fry the mushrooms for 5 minutes. Add the garlic and fry for another 2 minutes. Season to taste.

❧ Roll out the dough to two 20 cm/8 inch circles. Place on greased perforated pizza pans.

❧ Brush the dough with oil and spread with the tomato sauce. Add the mushrooms, and top with the green pepper.

❧ Bake in a preheated oven at 240°C/475°F/gas mark 9 for 15–20 minutes. Sprinkle with the Parmesan cheese, and garnish with torn basil leaves. Serve at once.

Artichoke and Cheese Pizza

MAKES ONE 30 CM/12 INCH PIZZA

1 quantity Basic Pizza Dough
Chilli Oil, for brushing
8 –10 bottled artichoke hearts, halved
salt and freshly ground black pepper

225 g/ 8 oz Emmenthal cheese,
  grated
3 tbsp freshly grated Parmesan
  cheese
basil leaves, to garnish

ROLL out the dough to a 30 cm/12 inch circle and place on a greased perforated pizza pan.

❧ Brush with chilli oil and arrange the artichoke hearts on top. Season to taste and top with the cheese.

❧ Bake in a preheated oven at 240°C/475°F/gas mark 9 for 15–20 minutes. Garnish with torn basil leaves, and serve immediately.

VARIATION: For Artichoke, Sun-Dried Tomato and Olive Pizza, top the cheese with 10–12 pitted black olives and 2 or 3 sliced sun-dried tomatoes.

Courgette Pizza with Rosemary

MAKES TWO 20 CM/8 INCH PIZZAS

3 tbsp olive oil
4 medium courgettes, halved
  lengthways and cut into 5 mm/
  ¼ inch slices
1 garlic clove, finely chopped
1½ tbsp finely chopped fresh rosemary

salt and freshly ground black pepper
1 quantity Basic Pizza Dough
225 g/8 oz mozzarella cheese, grated
6 black olives, pitted and halved
100 g/4 oz dry goat cheese, crumbled

HEAT the oil in a large frying pan, and fry the courgettes for 2 minutes. Add the garlic and 1 tablespoon of rosemary, and continue to fry until the courgettes are just coloured. Season with salt and pepper.

❧ Roll out the dough to two 20 cm/8 inch circles. Place on greased perforated pizza pans.

❧ Brush with olive oil. Sprinkle with mozzarella cheese, and arrange the courgettes and olives on top. Add the goat cheese and remaining rosemary.

❧ Bake in a preheated oven at 240°C/475°F/gas mark 9 for 15 minutes and serve at once.

Pizza Primavera

MAKES ONE 30 CM/12 INCH PIZZA

350 g/12 oz asparagus, trimmed
75 g/3 oz small courgettes, sliced
100 g/4 oz shelled small broad beans
1 quantity Basic Pizza Dough
olive oil, for brushing
225 g/8 oz mozzarella cheese, grated

salt and freshly ground black pepper
1 tbsp finely chopped fresh thyme
3 tbsp freshly grated Parmesan
    cheese
snipped fresh chives, to garnish

*S*TEAM the vegetables together over boiling water for 2 minutes. Rinse under cold water, and dry on absorbent kitchen paper. Cut off the asparagus tips, and chop the stalks roughly. Slip the outer skins off the broad beans.

❧ Roll out the dough to a 30 cm/12 inch circle. Transfer to a greased perforated pizza pan.

❧ Brush with oil, and sprinkle with the mozzarella cheese. Arrange the courgettes around the edge, then scatter over the broad beans, and asparagus stalks and tips. Sprinkle with thyme, and season to taste. Drizzle with olive oil.

❧ Bake in a preheated oven at 240°C/475°F/gas mark 9 for 15–20 minutes. Sprinkle with the Parmesan cheese, garnish with chives, and serve at once.

Fennel and Tomato Pizza

MAKES ONE 30 CM/12 INCH PIZZA

2 fennel bulbs, trimmed and thinly
    sliced lengthways
2 tbsp olive oil
salt and freshly ground black pepper
1 quantity Basic Pizza Dough
1 quantity Tomato Sauce
3 plum tomatoes, peeled, sliced,
    seeded and drained

2 tbsp finely chopped flat-leafed
    parsley
175 g/6 oz dry goat cheese, crumbled
4 tbsp freshly grated Parmesan
    cheese
chopped fennel leaves, to garnish

*G*ENTLY fry the fennel in the oil until soft and just beginning to colour. Season to taste.

❧ Roll out the dough to a 30 cm/12 inch circle. Transfer to a greased perforated pizza pan.

❧ Brush with olive oil, and spread with tomato sauce. Add the fennel and tomato slices. Sprinkle with parsley, and season to taste. Top with the goat cheese, and drizzle with olive oil.

❧ Bake in a preheated oven at 240°C/475°F/gas mark 9 for 15–20 minutes. Sprinkle with Parmesan cheese, garnish with fennel leaves, and serve at once.

Peperoni, Chicory and Olive Pizza

MAKES ONE 30 CM/12 INCH PIZZA

1 quantity Basic Pizza Dough
olive oil, for brushing
1 quantity Tomato Sauce
175 g/6 oz mozzarella cheese, grated
2 large plump heads chicory,
    sliced lengthways
75 g/3 oz peperoni, thinly sliced

salt and freshly ground black pepper
8 pitted black olives, halved
3 tbsp freshly grated Parmesan
    cheese
coarsely chopped fresh flat-leafed
    parsley, to garnish

ROLL out the dough to a 30 cm/12 inch circle. Transfer to a greased perforated pizza pan.

❧ Brush with olive oil, and spread with the tomato sauce. Sprinkle with the mozzarella cheese, and arrange the chicory on top. Place the peperoni in the gaps. Brush the chicory with oil. Season to taste, and scatter the olives over the top.

❧ Bake in a preheated oven at 240°C/475°F/gas mark 9 for 20 minutes. Sprinkle with Parmesan cheese, garnish with parsley, and serve immediately.

Prosciutto, Celery and Shallot Pizza

MAKES ONE 30 CM/12 INCH PIZZA

2 tbsp olive oil
25 g/1 oz butter
225 g/8 oz tender celery stalks,
    sliced diagonally into
    2.5 cm/1 inch pieces
8 shallots, peeled and halved
    lengthways
1 tsp each finely chopped fresh thyme,
    rosemary and sage
1 tbsp balsamic vinegar

½ tsp sugar
2 tbsp stock
salt and freshly ground black pepper
1 quantity Basic Pizza Dough
175 g/6 oz gruyère cheese, grated
50 g/2 oz prosciutto, cut into
    small strips
3 tbsp freshly grated Parmesan
    cheese
chopped celery leaves, to garnish

HEAT the oil and butter in a large pan. Add the celery and shallots, cover, and gently fry for 5 minutes. Add the herbs, vinegar, sugar, stock and seasoning. Raise the heat and stir-fry for 2 minutes, until brown and glazed.

❧ Roll out the dough to a 30 cm/12 inch circle. Transfer to a greased perforated pizza pan. Sprinkle with the gruyère cheese, then add the celery, shallots and prosciutto.

❧ Bake in a preheated oven at 240°C/475°F/gas mark 9 for 15–20 minutes. Sprinkle with Parmesan cheese, garnish with celery leaves, and serve immediately.

Quick Focaccia Pizza with Peperoni

SERVES 4–6

3 bottled red peppers,
  drained and diced
3 oil-cured, sun-dried tomatoes, diced
6 tbsp freshly grated Parmesan
  cheese
3 tbsp finely chopped fresh coriander
  or flat-leafed parsley

2 garlic cloves, finely chopped
salt and freshly ground black pepper
12 slices focaccia or ciabatta
  bread
75 g/3 oz peperoni, thinly sliced
olive oil, for sprinkling

COMBINE the peppers, sun-dried tomatoes, half the Parmesan cheese, the coriander or parsley, garlic, and salt and pepper.

❧ Put the bread on a greased baking sheet, and spread a little of the pepper mixture over each. Top with a few slices of peperoni. Sprinkle with the remaining cheese and a few drops of olive oil.

❧ Bake in a preheated oven at 240°C/475°F/gas mark 9 for 5–10 minutes until bubbling.

French Bread Pizza with Bacon

SERVES 4–6

225 g/8 oz back bacon
1 large long French stick
3 tbsp tomato purée
200 g/7 oz can chopped tomatoes,
  drained
1 tbsp finely chopped fresh oregano

salt and freshly ground black pepper
100 g/4 oz Cheddar cheese, grated
  or mozzarella cheese, sliced
pitted black olives, halved, to garnish

COOK the bacon under a preheated moderate grill until crisp. Cool, then crumble coarsely.

❧ Cut the French stick in half and slice each half horizontally. Place the 4 pieces under a preheated hot grill, and toast the cut sides until golden.

❧ Spread the tomato purée evenly over the toasted bread, and place the tomatoes on top. Sprinkle over the crumbled bacon and oregano. Season to taste. Arrange the cheese on top, and garnish with the olives.

❧ Place under a preheated moderate grill and cook for 10 minutes, until golden and bubbling. Serve immediately, cut into slices.

Middle Eastern Lamb and Mint Pizza

MAKES TWO 20 CM/8 INCH PIZZAS

2 tbsp oil
1 onion, finely chopped
225 g/8 oz lean minced lamb
1 garlic clove, crushed
½ tsp ground cumin
1 tsp coriander seeds, crushed
pinch of ground cloves

1 tbsp tomato purée
200 g/7 oz can chopped tomatoes
salt and freshly ground black pepper
1 quantity Rich Pizza Dough
Chilli Oil, for brushing
coarsely chopped fresh mint,
   to garnish

*H*EAT the oil in a frying pan, add the onion and gently fry until translucent. Stir in the lamb, and brown well. Add the garlic, spices, tomato purée and tomatoes and season to taste. Simmer over a low heat until the mixture is thick.

❧ Roll out the dough to two 20 cm/8 inch circles. Transfer to greased perforated pizza pans.

❧ Brush with chilli oil, and spread with the lamb mixture.

❧ Bake in a preheated oven at 240°C/475°F/gas mark 9 for 15–20 minutes. Garnish with mint, and serve at once.

Chicken Pizza Mexicana

MAKES ONE 30 CM/12 INCH PIZZA

300 g/11 oz boneless, skinless
   chicken, cut into 2 cm/¾ inch
   pieces
finely grated zest of 2 limes
1 tsp coriander seeds, crushed
2 tbsp olive oil
1 quantity Basic Pizza Dough
100 g/4 oz mozzarella cheese, grated
75 g/3 oz smoked cheese, grated
75 g/3 oz canned red kidney beans

75 g/3 oz frozen sweetcorn kernels,
   defrosted
1 fresh chilli, seeded and
   finely chopped
½ red onion, very thinly sliced
½ red pepper, very thinly sliced
salt and freshly ground black pepper
coarsely chopped fresh coriander,
   to garnish

*R*UB the chicken with lime zest and coriander seeds, then stir-fry in the oil for 3 minutes.

❧ Roll out the dough to a 30 cm/12 inch circle. Transfer to a greased perforated pizza pan.

❧ Sprinkle with the cheeses, then the drained and rinsed kidney beans, sweetcorn and chilli.

❧ Arrange the onion and pepper slices on top, along with the chicken. Drizzle with oil, and season to taste.

❧ Bake in a preheated oven at 240°C/475°F/gas mark 9 for 20–25 minutes. Garnish with coriander, and serve immediately.

Peperoni and Mushroom Pizza

MAKES ONE 25 × 35 CM/10 × 14 INCH PIZZA

3 tbsp olive oil
3 onions, thinly sliced
1 garlic clove, finely chopped
2 × 400 g/14 oz cans chopped
    tomatoes
2 tbsp finely chopped fresh mixed
    herbs

1 tbsp tomato purée
salt and freshly ground black pepper
1 quantity Basic Pizza Dough
100 g/4 oz button mushrooms,
    thinly sliced
175 g/6 oz mozzarella cheese, grated
100g/4 oz peperoni, thinly sliced

HEAT the oil in a frying pan, and gently fry the onion for 5 minutes, until soft and lightly coloured. Stir in the garlic, chopped tomatoes, herbs and tomato purée, and season to taste. Bring to the boil, then lower the heat and simmer for 20–30 minutes until thickened. Remove from the heat and leave to cool.

❧ Roll out the dough to a 25 × 35 cm/10 × 14 inch rectangle. Transfer to a greased Swiss roll tin.

❧ Spoon the tomato mixture evenly over the dough, and scatter with the mushrooms. Sprinkle with the mozzarella cheese, and arrange the peperoni on top.

❧ Bake in a preheated oven at 240°C/475°F/gas mark 9 for 20 minutes. Serve immediately.

Fried Pizza with Egg and Bacon

MAKES FOUR 12.5 CM/5 INCH PIZZAS

8 rashers streaky bacon
1 quantity Basic Pizza Dough
    (unrisen if short of time)
olive oil, for frying

½ quantity Tomato Sauce or
    8 tbsp passata
4 eggs
salt and freshly ground black pepper
2 tbsp finely chopped parsley

GRILL the bacon until crisp, cut in half crossways, and keep warm.

❧ Roll out the dough to four 12.5 cm/5 inch circles.

❧ In a large, heavy-based pan, heat enough oil to come just level with the tops of the circles. Fry the circles for about 5 minutes until pale golden on the under side.

❧ Turn over, spread with tomato sauce or passata, and fry the second side. Remove from the pan and keep warm.

❧ Fry the eggs in the same pan.

❧ Arrange the bacon and eggs on top of the bases. Season to taste, sprinkle with parsley, and serve at once.

Spicy Chicken Pizza

MAKES ONE 30 CM/12 INCH PIZZA

350 g/12 oz boneless, skinless
chicken, cut into 2 cm/¾ inch
pieces
2 tbsp olive oil
salt and freshly ground black pepper
1 quantity Basic Pizza Dough
Chilli Oil, for brushing
1 quantity Tomato Sauce
4 tbsp chopped fresh coriander
75 g/3 oz feta cheese, crumbled

MARINADE:
100 ml/3½ fl oz Greek yogurt
2 garlic cloves, crushed
2.5 cm/1 inch piece fresh ginger root,
finely chopped
¼ tsp chilli powder
1 tsp cumin seeds, crushed
salt and freshly ground black pepper

COMBINE the marinade ingredients with the chicken. Cover and refrigerate for at least 4 hours or overnight.

❧ Heat the oil and stir-fry the chicken for 3 minutes.

❧ Roll out the dough to a 30 cm/12 inch circle. Transfer to a greased perforated pizza pan.

❧ Brush with chilli oil, and spread with the tomato sauce. Sprinkle with 3 tablespoons of the coriander. Top with the chicken, followed by the feta cheese. Drizzle with chilli oil.

❧ Bake in a preheated oven at 240°C/475°F/gas mark 9 for 15–20 minutes. Garnish with the remaining coriander, and serve immediately.

Barbecued Chicken Pizza

MAKES ONE 30 CM/12 INCH PIZZA

350 g/12 oz boneless, skinless
chicken, cut into 2 cm/¾ inch
pieces
175 ml/6 fl oz barbecue sauce
2 tbsp olive oil

1 quantity Basic Pizza Dough
75 g/3 oz Cheddar cheese, grated
100 g/4 oz mozzarella cheese, grated
1 small red onion, very thinly sliced
marjoram leaves, to garnish

COMBINE the chicken with half the barbecue sauce. Cover and refrigerate for at least 4 hours or overnight.

❧ Heat the olive oil and stir-fry the chicken for 3 minutes.

❧ Roll out the dough to a 30 cm/12 inch circle. Transfer to a greased perforated pizza pan.

❧ Spread with the remaining barbecue sauce. Sprinkle evenly with the cheeses. Arrange the chicken and the onion rings on top, and sprinkle with a little oil.

❧ Bake in a preheated oven at 240°C/475°F/gas mark 9 for 15–20 minutes. Garnish with marjoram, and serve immediately.

Salami and Anchovy Pizza

MAKES ONE 30 CM/12 INCH PIZZA

1 quantity Basic Pizza Dough
olive oil, for brushing
1 quantity Tomato Sauce
100 g/4 oz salami, thinly sliced

100 g/4 oz mozzarella cheese,
   thinly sliced
50 g/2 oz can anchovy fillets, drained
10 black olives, pitted

*R*OLL out the dough to a 30 cm/12 inch circle, and place on a greased perforated pizza pan.

❦ Brush with oil and spread the tomato sauce evenly over the dough. Cover with the salami slices. Arrange the sliced cheese on top. Make a lattice with the anchovy fillets, and scatter over the olives. Drizzle with olive oil.

❦ Bake in a preheated oven at 240°C/475°F/gas mark 9 for 15–20 minutes. Serve immediately.

Ricotta, Ham and Sage Pizza

MAKES ONE 30 CM/12 INCH PIZZA

1 quantity Rich Pizza Dough
350 g/12 oz ricotta or curd cheese,
   sieved
3 tbsp freshly grated Parmesan
   cheese

1 large egg, beaten
75 g/3 oz cooked ham, diced
3 tbsp finely chopped fresh sage
salt and freshly ground black pepper
basil leaves, to garnish

*R*OLL out the dough to a 30 cm/12 inch circle, and place on a greased perforated pizza pan.

❦ Beat together the cheeses and the egg. Mix in the ham and sage, and season to taste. Spread the cheese mixture evenly over the dough.

❦ Bake in a preheated oven at 240°C/475°F/gas mark 9 for 15–20 minutes. Garnish with basil leaves, and serve at once.

Pancetta, Leek and Green Peppercorn Pizzette

MAKES FOUR 15 CM/6 INCH PIZZAS

1 quantity Basic Pizza Dough
olive oil, for brushing
75 g/3 oz mozzarella cheese, grated
75 g/3 oz Cheddar cheese, grated
1 tsp green peppercorns

1 leek, halved lengthways and
  thinly sliced
6 slices pancetta (or smoked streaky
bacon), sliced into 7.5 cm/3 inch
  pieces
snipped chives, to garnish

*R*OLL out the dough to four 15 cm/6 inch circles. Transfer to greased perforated pizza pans.

❧ Brush with olive oil, and sprinkle with the cheeses and green peppercorns. Top with the leeks and pancetta.

❧ Bake in a preheated oven at 240°C/475°F/gas mark 9 for 12–15 minutes. Garnish with chives, and serve immediately.

Pizza Quattro Stagioni
(Four Seasons Pizza)

MAKES ONE 30 CM/12 INCH PIZZA

3 tbsp olive oil
50 g/2 oz button mushrooms, sliced
1 quantity Basic Pizza Dough
50 g/2 oz Parma ham, cut into strips
6 pitted black olives, thinly sliced

4 bottled artichoke hearts,
  drained and thinly sliced
50 g/2 oz mozzarella cheese, sliced
1 tomato, peeled, seeded and sliced
salt and freshly ground black pepper

*H*EAT the olive oil in a frying pan and stir-fry the mushrooms for 5 minutes.

❧ Roll out the dough to a 30 cm/12 inch circle, and place on a greased perforated pizza pan. Brush with olive oil, and mark it into 4 sections with the back of a knife.

❧ Place the mushrooms on one of the marked sections. Place the ham in the second section, and top with the olives. Arrange the artichoke hearts in the third section, and the mozzarella and tomato slices in the fourth. Season to taste, and drizzle with olive oil.

❧ Bake in a preheated oven at 240°C/475°F/gas mark 9 for 15–20 minutes. Serve immediately, cut into wedges.

Pastrami and Rye Pizza

MAKES ONE 30 CM/12 INCH PIZZA

1 quantity Basic Pizza Dough,
    made with 175 g/6 oz strong plain
    flour and 50 g/2 oz rye flour
1 quantity Tomato Sauce
olive oil, for brushing
100 g/4 oz mozzarella cheese,
    grated

100 g/4 oz gruyère cheese, grated
50 g/2 oz pastrami, cut into
    5 cm/2 inch pieces
½ red onion, diced
½ green pepper, seeded and diced
salt and freshly ground black pepper
3 tbsp freshly grated Parmesan
    cheese

*R*OLL out the dough to a 30 cm/12 inch circle. Transfer to a greased perforated pizza pan.

❧ Brush with olive oil, and spread with the tomato sauce. Sprinkle with the gruyère and mozzarella cheeses. Add the pastrami and scatter over the onion and pepper. Season to taste and sprinkle with olive oil.

❧ Bake in a preheated oven at 240°C/475°F/gas mark 9 for 15 minutes. Sprinkle with Parmesan cheese, and serve immediately.

Pancetta and Olive Pizza

MAKES ONE 30 CM/12 INCH PIZZA

1 quantity Basic Pizza Dough
olive oil, for brushing
1 quantity Tomato Sauce
225 g/8 oz mozzarella cheese,
    grated

8 slices of pancetta (or smoked
    streaky bacon)
8 black olives, pitted and halved
finely chopped parsley, to garnish

*R*OLL out the dough to a 30 cm/12 inch circle. Transfer to a greased perforated pizza pan.

❧ Brush the dough with oil, and spread evenly with the tomato sauce. Sprinkle with mozzarella, and arrange the bacon on top like the spokes of a wheel. Top with olive halves.

❧ Bake in a preheated oven at 240°C/475°F/gas mark 9 for 15–20 minutes. Garnish with the parsley and serve immediately.

Peperoni and Prosciutto Pizza

MAKES TWO 20 CM/8 INCH PIZZAS

1 large onion, thinly sliced
1 tbsp olive oil
225 g/8 oz prosciutto, thinly sliced
100 g/4 oz peperoni, thinly sliced
1 quantity Basic Pizza Dough
1 quantity Tomato Sauce

2 tbsp finely chopped fresh
   marjoram
salt and freshly ground black pepper
3 tbsp freshly grated Parmesan
   cheese

*G*ENTLY fry the onion in the oil until golden. Remove from the heat, and stir in the prosciutto and peperoni.

❦ Roll out the dough to two 20 cm/8 inch circles. Place on greased perforated pizza pans.

❦ Spread the tomato sauce over the dough, and cover with the onion mixture. Sprinkle with marjoram, and season to taste.

❦ Bake in a preheated oven at 240°C/475°F/gas mark 9 for 15–20 minutes. Sprinkle with Parmesan, and serve at once.

Antipasto Pizzette

MAKES FOUR 12.5 CM/5 INCH PIZZAS

1 quantity Basic Pizza Dough
olive oil, for brushing
1 quantity Tomato Sauce
100g/4 oz peperoni, thinly sliced
7 black olives, pitted and halved
1 tsp capers, drained
2 tbsp freshly grated Parmesan
   cheese

6 slices salami
6 green olives, pitted
50 g/2 oz gruyère cheese, sliced
1 oil-cured, sun-dried tomato, cut into
   strips
50 g/2 oz mozzarella cheese, sliced
6 anchovy fillets

*R*OLL out the dough to four 12.5 cm/5 inch circles. Place on a greased perforated pizza pan. Brush with olive oil, and spread the tomato sauce evenly over the dough.

❦ Place two-thirds of the peperoni slices in the centre of one circle and top with six of the black olives and the capers. Sprinkle with Parmesan cheese.

❦ Shape the salami slices into cones, and arrange them on the second dough circle. Top with the green olives.

❦ Place the gruyère cheese and sun-dried tomato in the centre of the third circle, with the remaining peperoni around the edge.

❦ Arrange the mozzarella cheese on the fourth circle, and place the anchovies on top with the remaining black olive.

❦ Leave to rise for 15–30 minutes. Bake in a preheated oven at 240°C/475°F/gas mark 9 for 15 minutes, and serve immediately.

Chorizo and Lentil Pizza

MAKES TWO 20 CM/8 INCH PIZZAS

75 g/3 oz lentils de Puy
  (or green lentils)
1 tbsp olive oil
1 small onion, finely chopped
2 garlic cloves, finely chopped
1 small fresh green chilli,
  seeded and finely chopped
½ tsp cumin seeds, crushed
1 tbsp tomato purée

200 g/7 oz can chopped tomatoes
2 tbsp chopped fresh flat-leafed
  parsley or fresh coriander
salt and freshly ground black pepper
1 quantity Rich Pizza Dough
40 g/1½ oz thinly sliced chorizo
  (Spanish sausage), cut into segments
chopped fresh mint, to garnish

COOK the lentils in boiling water for about 10 minutes, until just tender. Drain and set aside.

❧ Heat the oil in a saucepan, and gently fry the onion until translucent. Stir in the garlic, chilli, cumin and tomato purée. Fry for another minute, then add the chopped tomatoes and parsley. Add the lentils, season to taste, and simmer for 5 minutes until thickened slightly.

❧ Roll out the dough to two 20 cm/8 inch circles. Transfer to greased perforated pizza pans.

❧ Brush with olive oil, and spread the lentil mixture over the dough. Arrange the chorizo slices on top.

❧ Bake in a preheated oven at 240°C/475°F/gas mark 9 for 12–15 minutes. Garnish with mint, and serve warm or cold.

Italian Sausage Pizza

MAKES ONE 30 CM/12 INCH PIZZA

1 quantity Basic Pizza Dough
olive oil, for brushing
1 quantity Tomato Sauce
100 g/4 oz Italian sausage, sliced
225 g/8 oz mozzarella cheese,
  grated

4 tbsp freshly grated Parmesan
  cheese
3 slices cooked ham, cut into strips
8 black olives, pitted
1 tbsp chopped fresh flat-leafed
  parsley, to garnish

ROLL out the dough to a 30 cm/12 inch circle, and place on a greased perforated pizza pan.

❧ Brush with oil, and spread the tomato sauce evenly over the dough. Arrange the sausage on top and sprinkle with mozzarella and Parmesan cheeses. Arrange the ham in a lattice, with the olives in the spaces. Drizzle with olive oil.

❧ Bake in a preheated oven at 240°C/475°F/gas mark 9 for 20 minutes. Garnish with parsley and serve at once.

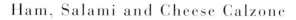

Ham, Salami and Cheese Calzone

MAKES ONE 30 CM/12 INCH CALZONE

1 quantity Rich Pizza Dough
olive oil, for brushing
150 g/5 oz ricotta cheese, sieved
40 g/1½ oz Parmesan cheese,
   grated
1 small egg

1 tbsp finely chopped fresh sage
salt and freshly ground pepper
50 g/2 oz ham or prosciutto, diced
25 g/1 oz thinly sliced salami,
   peeled and cut into strips
100 g/4 oz mozzarella cheese, diced

ROLL out the dough to a 30–33 cm/12–13 inch circle. Place on a greased perforated pizza pan. Brush the middle of the dough with oil, and moisten the edge with water.

❧ Combine the ricotta and Parmesan with the egg, sage and seasoning. Spread the mixture over half the circle. Arrange the ham and salami on top, then add the mozzarella.

❧ Fold over the dough to make a semi-circle, pressing the edges firmly together. Brush with olive oil.

❧ Bake in a preheated oven at 220°C/425°F/gas mark 7 for 30–35 minutes, until golden. Brush with oil. Cut into wedges and serve warm.

Pancetta and New Potato Pizza

MAKES TWO 20 CM/8 INCH PIZZAS

275 g/10 oz small waxy new potatoes,
   unpeeled
2 tbsp olive oil
2 garlic cloves, finely chopped
1½ tbsp finely chopped fresh
   rosemary
salt and freshly ground black pepper

1 quantity Basic Pizza Dough
75 g/3 oz smoked cheese, grated
75 g/3 oz gruyère cheese, grated
75 g/3 oz pancetta (or smoked
   streaky bacon), cut into 1.5 cm/¾
   inch pieces
8 pitted black olives, halved

BLANCH the potatoes in boiling salted water for 3 minutes. Drain, allow to cool, then slice thinly.

❧ Heat the olive oil in a large frying pan. Fry the potatoes, with the garlic and 1 tablespoon of rosemary, for 3–4 minutes, carefully turning the potato slices. Season with salt and pepper.

❧ Roll out the dough to two 20 cm/8 inch circles. Transfer to greased perforated pizza pans.

❧ Sprinkle with about two-thirds of the cheeses. Arrange the potatoes on top, followed by the remaining cheese. Top with the pancetta, olives and remaining rosemary.

❧ Bake in a preheated oven at 240°C/475°F/gas mark 9 for 15–20 minutes. Serve at once.

Tuna, Tomato and Anchovy Pizza

MAKES ONE 30 × 23 CM/12 × 9 INCH PIZZA

1 quantity Basic Wholemeal Dough
olive oil, for brushing
200 g/7 oz can tuna fish, drained
1½ quantities Tomato Sauce

50 g/2 oz can anchovies, drained
175 g/6 oz Emmenthal cheese, grated
12 black olives, pitted
finely chopped parsley, to garnish

ROLL out the dough to a 30 × 23 cm/12 × 9 inch rectangle. Transfer to a greased Swiss roll tin, and brush the dough with oil.

❧ Mash the tuna with a fork, and spread it evenly over the dough. Spread the tomato sauce evenly over the fish. Arrange the anchovy fillets diagonally on top, and sprinkle with the cheese. Top with the olives.

❧ Bake in a preheated oven at 240°C/475°F/gas mark 9 for 15–20 minutes, until the cheese is bubbling. Garnish with parsley and cut into squares.

Prawn, Mushroom and Sweetcorn Pizza

MAKES ONE 30 CM/12 INCH PIZZA

2 tbsp olive oil
225 g/8 oz button mushrooms,
    thinly sliced
1 garlic clove, finely chopped
2 tbsp finely chopped parsley
salt and freshly ground black pepper
1 quantity Basic Pizza Dough
1 quantity Tomato Sauce

75 g/3 oz frozen sweetcorn kernels,
    defrosted
1–2 tsp capers, drained
150 g/5 oz large peeled prawns
175 g/6 oz mozzarella cheese, diced
finely chopped fresh mixed herbs,
    to garnish

HEAT the oil in a frying pan and stir-fry the mushrooms for 5 minutes. Stir in the garlic and parsley, and fry for another minute. Season to taste, and leave to cool.

❧ Roll out the dough to a 30 cm/12 inch circle, and place on a greased perforated pizza pan.

❧ Brush with oil, and spread the tomato sauce evenly over the dough.

❧ Bake in a preheated oven at 240°C/475°F/gas mark 9 for 15 minutes. Remove from the oven.

❧ Arrange the mushrooms on top. Sprinkle with the sweetcorn kernels and capers. Top with the prawns and cheese. Drizzle with olive oil.

❧ Bake for 5–7 minutes more, until the cheese has melted. Garnish with herbs, and serve immediately.

Pizza Frutti di Mare
(Seafood Pizza)

MAKES ONE 30 CM/12 INCH PIZZA

450 g/1 lb mixed cooked seafood
   e.g. squid, cockles, clams,
   mussels, prawns
grated zest of ½ lemon
2 garlic cloves, finely chopped
3 tbsp olive oil
cayenne pepper

salt and freshly ground black pepper
1 quantity Basic Pizza Dough
1 quantity Tomato Sauce
6 tbsp freshly grated Parmesan
   cheese
basil leaves, to garnish

Put the seafood in a bowl with the lemon zest, garlic, olive oil, cayenne, and salt and pepper. Marinate for 30 minutes.

❧ Roll out the dough to a 30 cm/12 inch circle. Place on a greased perforated pizza pan.

❧ Brush with olive oil, and spread with the tomato sauce.

❧ Bake in a preheated oven at 240°C/475°F/gas mark 9 for 15 minutes.

❧ Remove from the oven, and arrange the seafood on top. Sprinkle with 4 tablespoons of Parmesan cheese.

❧ Bake for 7–10 minutes more, until the seafood is heated through. Sprinkle with the remaining Parmesan cheese, garnish with basil leaves, and serve at once.

Smoked Salmon and
Mascarpone Pizzette

MAKES SIX 12.5 CM/5 INCH PIZZAS

250 g/9 oz mascarpone cheese
2 shallots, finely chopped
1 tbsp lemon juice
2 tbsp finely chopped fresh dill
salt and freshly ground black pepper

1 quantity Rich Pizza Dough
olive oil, for brushing
175 g/6 oz smoked salmon,
   cut into narrow strips
dill leaves, to garnish

Combine the mascarpone cheese, shallots, lemon juice, dill, and seasoning.

❧ Roll out the dough to six 12.5 cm/5 inch circles. Place on greased perforated pizza pans.

❧ Brush with olive oil, and spread with the cheese mixture.

❧ Bake in a preheated oven at 240°C/475°F/gas mark 9 for 15 minutes. Remove from the oven, and arrange the smoked salmon on top. Garnish with dill leaves, and serve at once.

Spicy Prawn Pizza

MAKES TWO 20 CM/8 INCH PIZZAS

200 g/7 oz large shelled prawns	½ tsp cumin seeds
2 tbsp lime juice	½ tsp coriander seeds
3 tbsp olive oil	1 onion, finely chopped
2 garlic cloves, crushed	400 g/14 oz can chopped tomatoes
2.5 cm/1 inch piece fresh root ginger, very finely chopped	½ tsp salt
⅛–¼ tsp cayenne pepper	1 quantity Basic Pizza Dough
1 tsp turmeric	coarsely chopped fresh coriander, to garnish

SPRINKLE the prawns with 1 tablespoon each of the lime juice and olive oil.

❧ Combine the garlic, ginger and spices with 1 tablespoon of the olive oil, and mash together to a paste.

❧ Heat the remaining oil and fry the onion until golden. Add the spice paste and fry for 1 minute. Add the tomatoes, salt, and remaining lime juice. Simmer for 5 minutes until thick.

❧ Roll out the dough to two 20 cm/8 inch circles. Place on greased perforated pizza pans. Brush with olive oil, spread with the tomato mixture, and sprinkle with oil.

❧ Bake in a preheated oven at 240°C/ 475°F/gas mark 9 for 15 minutes. Arrange the prawns on top and bake for 4–5 minutes more, until the prawns are heated through. Garnish with coriander, and serve at once.

Sardine and Leek Pizza

MAKES ONE 30 CM/12 INCH PIZZA

1 quantity Basic Pizza Dough	100 g/4 oz feta cheese, crumbled
olive oil, for brushing	salt and freshly ground black pepper
1 quantity Tomato Sauce	1 tbsp finely chopped fresh rosemary
8 fresh sardines, cleaned and boned	
2 medium leeks, halved lengthways and thinly sliced	

ROLL out the dough to a 30 cm/12 inch circle. Place on a greased perforated pizza pan. Brush with olive oil, and spread with the tomato sauce.

❧ Bake in a preheated oven at 240°C/475°F/gas mark 9 for 12 minutes. Arrange the sardines on top, like the spokes of a wheel. Sprinkle the leeks and feta cheese in the gaps. Season to taste, and sprinkle with rosemary.

❧ Bake for 8 minutes more, and serve at once.

Pizza alla Calabrese

MAKES ONE 30 CM/12 INCH PIZZA

2 tbsp olive oil
1 onion, finely chopped
400 g/14 oz can chopped tomatoes
2 garlic cloves, finely chopped
salt and freshly ground black pepper
175 g/6 oz can tuna fish in oil,
 undrained

6 anchovy fillets, chopped
1 tbsp capers, drained
1 quantity Basic Pizza Dough
12 oz pitted black olives
chopped fresh flat-leafed parsley,
 to garnish

*H*EAT the oil in a frying pan, and gently fry the onion for 2–3 minutes. Add the tomatoes and garlic, and season to taste. Simmer over a low heat for 5 minutes until thickened. Add the tuna fish, anchovies and capers.

❧ Roll out the dough to a 30 cm/12 inch circle, and place on a greased perforated pizza pan.

❧ Brush with olive oil. Spread the tuna mixture evenly over the top. Drizzle with more olive oil, and top with the olives.

❧ Bake in a preheated oven at 240°C/475°F/gas mark 9 for 15 minutes. Lower the oven temperature to 190°C/375°F/gas mark 5 and bake for a further 10 minutes. Garnish with parsley, and serve immediately.

Mediterranean Fish Pizza

MAKES ONE 30 CM/12 INCH PIZZA

350 g/12 oz halibut or cod, skinned
 and cut into bite-sized chunks
juice of ½ lemon
Garlic Oil, for brushing
salt and freshly ground black pepper
1 quantity Basic Pizza Dough
1 quantity Tomato Sauce

1 green pepper, seeded and
 very thinly sliced
3 plum tomatoes, peeled, sliced
 and seeded
12–14 pitted black olives
1 tsp dried oregano
marjoram leaves, to garnish

*S*PRINKLE the fish with lemon juice, garlic oil, salt and pepper, and leave to marinate for at least 2 hours.

❧ Roll out the dough to a 30 cm/12 inch circle. Place on a greased perforated pizza pan. Brush with garlic oil, spread with the tomato sauce, and arrange the peppers and tomatoes on top. Sprinkle with oregano and oil.

❧ Bake in a preheated oven at 240°C/475°F/gas mark 9 for 20 minutes. Drain the fish, and arrange on top, together with the olives. Bake for 5 minutes more, until the fish is just cooked. Garnish with marjoram and serve at once.